A CRUISE IN
RARE WATERS

Poems by
Sara M. Robinson

Cedar Creek Publishing
Bremo Bluff, Virginia
www.cedarcreekauthors.com

Printed in the United States of America

ISBN 978-0-9839192-9-2

TABLE OF CONTENTS

I Wear These Old Symbols

Weathered beach glass earrings
A totem of ancient tribes on a string

And I feel a
People who once
Held them in other forms
With dreams of
Their own destinies

Or perhaps a wish
For a new day

I see my friends
And we touch
A glass together
Or admire some
Special snowfall

When a thousand
Years from this
Moment a wanderer
Picks up a satin
Shard and turns it over

Will he feel us

In the House of All Clans

In the smoke-filled tent
hides of walrus define
perimeters which guard
against laws of nature
and provide cover over
man who attempts to
create his own natural laws

From the discovery of
mountains   rivers
shores   and   otters
tribes set down
their roots and claimed
everything they could
see as their own

In language formed
from Russian   French
and   archaic cave-dweller
utterings these people
designed their own
destiny and spoke
to gods they knew
protected them   fed them
nursed them   killed them

Their totems carved
from grandfather trees
told of their heritage
and their respect of
mighty crows   soaring eagles
silver salmon   majestic brown bears

Then outsiders came

A Cruise in Rare Waters

We're greeted with
scents of exotic spices as
grilling of salmon sifts
through open doors
to a promenade on
this ship sailing

at every station
for every hand the
dispenser of cold
hand sanitizer greets
those who would prefer
not to touch anyway

the beauty of northern
semi-frozen waters
is exposed to spectators
who strain to see
some native species and
remain hopeful that
none will be gone
in this lifetime

how desperate we
must seem as
outsiders even as
mammals are leaving
and birds disappear

while glaciers recede
and what little
ice remains is soiled

on this inside passage
we can only touch
some of what
we see and at that
with purified hands

I Prefer My Ice Shaken

I have no cause
to pick vodka or gin
I can shake or stir
from the front or
back seat–close in
or close out

the parts–whether heads
or tails–are the same
fronts or backs are
disturbed either way
all keep moving

the scents of exotic
fragrance or the
grilling of fish take
to the air whether
it is here or through
an open door to
a railing of some vessel
cutting   raking

through cold–very cold–
you might say–
crushed icy water
where the beauty of
this lies in big truths
like rites of passage

whether the truths
are big or small
the spectators and
participants will see
them for what they are

and I will say I could
have taken this inside
passage or the open sea
but I chose eventually
to do neither because

the truth is I would
just rather drink
the icy mix and
watch the frost
slide down–
        so   slowly down
            the inside window

On Being in the Wild Place

It's cold on the last
train of the season
and we gasp at
sightings of mountain goats
and tombstones

rivers rush by and
their golden sands
lie silent in luster
no longer mined

under rubble piles
we learn lie bones
of horses and a few men—
an ancestor of our conductor
worked at laying the track

we climb across steep grades
on match stick supports
around curves only
narrow gauge would fit

it's a mysterious passage
the clack   clack of wheels
the darkness of tunnels
the smell   the heat
of a woodstove in front

I shiver like some
ghost walked over my grave
and cannot shake off
any remaining skin

Inside Passage

When the ship edged
Through the narrow passage
Clothed in darkness
Like a tomb that waits

I missed the event
As I slid through dreams
Captured in our cabin

Any creaking or groaning
Was masked by soundings
Against walls of unseen height
In waters of unknown depth

Later, Filipino workers
Looked for wounds
While I examined skin
Cruising awfully near
A lightning bolt

Corrections

The mountains are vast
too large to describe
too jagged to touch
with their hanging glaciers
ice shelves   overall cragginess

we sat at the bar
with our crystal clear
drinks–smallest shallow
waters and talked of
deep waters   frozen waters

what I took as a souvenir
one memento that was
more than a moment
more than a small record
a smooth speckled rock
in my hand

this big big land
me   this small   small   person
who can only see the
mountain animals in
my mind's eye

save for some white dots
far enough away
to my naked eye where
they look like
correction fluid drops
on jagged lines of text

Dining Quietly

While we were gone
a snap broke a neck
of another who reached
for some small seed

not quick enough
jaws faster than sound
stopped the action

while we dined
on the fourth day
at yet another buffet
of assorted grains and fishes
our hands holding plates
extended for seconds

and accompanied by
laughs and words of
a large convergence
of similar doing all
the same things
no solitary unnecessary dining

and one solitary little beast
trying to feast as well
counted a small number
of seeds just close enough
with one more slight move
did not see the
danger of the reach

A Word is Breached

To find this right word
To sound to a depth
To rise into perfect
Placement bound into
The beating heart
Of a small poem

Is a surfacing humpback
About to get its fill
Of krill in frothing water
And which too presses
Fumes out of majestic filters
Watched by kayakers
Who draw closer and   closer
Only to see everything as fish

Fjord

These islands of ice
Chiseled blue-white clouds
Float in midnight waters
Color so blue   so cold
I cannot name it
But I can feel it and I

Hear them choking the fjord
Their squeaks and cracks
Speak of a strain to keep
Moving their bobbing tops
And their bigger bottoms

The ship dodges them
As if in a child's game
Spraying ice water across
The bow where crystals
Hang like so many stars

Brilliant in a sun
Before they fall
Back to water
To freeze and resume
Their continuous churning

They move away from us
A retreat perhaps or
Resumption of their journey
To a salted sea where they
Will catch up with others
And head for wider oceans

As we glide closer to the mother
We see more of her offspring
Then know we can go no further
Our quest must now divert
For the narrowness can trap us
If we linger too long

The struggle within a maternal canal
As the ship makes a complete full
Turn takes us back to the outside
Where all the water seems large
And small but will become
The very nature of all of us

                    Of all of us

Glacial Recession

It's not enough
    To guess your
        Extraordinary weight

You've gathered this
    Stone-by-stone
        Ice mass-by-ice mass

For eons without the interference
Of man and his fancy brain

We don't appreciate
    All your hard work
        So in our heated
            Climate–caused sanctum
Created by our own
    Hot words and
        Sulfuric industrial gases

Don't spare us
    Any mercy
        In your recession

The Shade of Arctic Blue

The water dressed
in foam hats jogs
behind us in froths
and swells which
end with the sky

The color of the
sea pulls me
into this space

where I taste
hundreds of shades
of blue hidden
within their thousands
of names and I

want to find one
that describes how
this water makes
me feel but

I cannot drink
the color I want–
I'm too far below
the surface where
the only blue
I see is black

Continued...

And this ink
is too thick
too old
too salty
on my tongue

Ketchikan Creek

I think Ketchikan Creek saved
my poetry which needed
a Good Samaritan

when we were in Ketchikan
I saw my words lying
in a creek bed
Salmon swam right over them
people walked right by them
no one noticed if
my words were still alive

but they were
waiting patiently for rescue
like a cedar log waits
for a carver to make
the bear hold a fish
to present to the thunderbird

at the house of
clans those who
enter will either
feel the gods
or will simply
be glad to be
out of the weather

Prayers for a Salmon Run

Quiet harbor hugs
a coastline framed
by tall trees and

low flying clouds
where a river keeps
order for most of the year

once canneries and
saloons held natives
captive by riches
and by vices

all lived and died
for the silver linings
and cardinal shades

of those fishes
whose presence was
worshipped and whose
absence was feared

the fervent and regular
prayers to St. Therese
begged always for
the best run
of salmon every year

the little catholic church
built next to the last ladder
offered up its own liturgy
for fishers of men
and men who fish
casting lines and nets
both seeking a
hot fishing spot

Salmon Spawn

They run cafes,
shops selling trinkets
for cruise ships
cheap jewelry with
wire and pieces of
local rocks and bark

They count inventory
of miniature plastic
totem poles   authentic
Made in China

They wear Nikes and
hoodies from Target
that say Property of
Fairbanks Juvenile Hall

Their straight hair
cut short is no longer
called raven–it's just black

No ceremonial feathers
or exotic leathers are donned
All replaced by Justin Bieber
t-shirts and Lady Gaga tights

But they are still
Alaskans under all
those garments
in their skin

and we are still
outsiders in ours

What we take
in our bags when
we leave is not really
of them
They rise out of waters
again and again these
children of salmon

Stratified Poetry

Trolling through icy waters
I lift my binoculars
to examine towering rock
formations rising
some two hundred feet
beside the bow.

I feel the rocks
hard   cold   resistant.
I sense small
waves knocking against
secrets. The erosion
will take its toll
a few grains at a time.
Stones will fall long
after I've left.

I hear the rocks'
low sounds
like an elephant
matriarch who keeps
her tribe together.

Stones move against
each other speaking
to themselves reciting
their own poetry.

In a hidden zone
precious metal sleeps
buried   captured
maybe never to
be liberated.

Tableau Vivant

Icebergs stilled by
the ship's passing
compete in frozen silence
for space

Neither will yield
willingly but choke
loudly their dismay

Moments later we
hear the captain
announce in controlled anger
that It's too dangerous
we must turn around

I hear icebergs
cracking off
port side in their
victory dance which
seems too close
as if two buccaneers
locked their swords

Both drop their
egos and resume
their fights with
lesser foes

Veuve Cliquot

The clarity of the amber
as it sparkles in its
escape route seemed
like another amber
which holds a scarab
captured in a time capsule

We took our glasses
out to the deck
hoisted our hands
to celebrate our
landing and our
ending of this
wilderness trek

What early explorers
must have seen
we can only imagine
from our comfort
but we are under
the same sky
We breathe the
same air

Bubbles escape into
the same space where
ones walked or sailed
in certain less comfort
than us and we still
call ourselves adventurers

Sticks and Stones

Ancient tribes used sticks
to traverse cliffs high
crevasses low and deep
measuring depths of
handholds   finding bats
These sticks they carried
were sturdy and priceless

In their travels
tribesmen sought the land
and their food with
other sticks   the pointed ones
which the black bear saw
from his retreat

Hidden he saw white hairless
Flesh   reflecting back the sun
He looked at his own
skin and saw something
familiar on the hairless one
hides of some animals
which he knew from his roaming

The white man walked upright
carried sticks   the pointed ones
The bear watched him
He picked up a scent
Harsh   acrid   not sweet
like his blueberries

Before he ever saw his
first person the bear
knew he would find challenge
(not for a mate) but
for the land

Winds blow through days
and long nights
Sticks explore cracks
find soft beating spots
And always at dawn
a journey starts again

It Was Alaska

We finished the towns
we crossed canyons
        and snaking deep rivers
we gaped at hanging
glaciers with their
        icy remoteness
we plowed through
water of such blue
that only ones who
were from there
could describe the
color and make you
feel you were marooned

The mountains with their
granite and metamorphic
stones held together a place
so distant and vague that
I feared failure in my
attempts to write words
which could tell of its
history with any kind
of pioneering clarity

I was a stranger
to this land
squeezed in between
salmon runs and mine tailings

I would never know
the layers and layers
of mankind who formed
native ways and spoke
of how these ways
touched outsiders like myself

This land would never
give me what I left there
            it was raw   sharp   vulnerable

It was Alaska

www.ingramcontent.com/pod-product-compliance
Lightning Source LLC
Chambersburg PA
CBHW051001030426
42339CB00007B/439